Design a Home for a Pet

by Becky Manfredini

HOUGHTON MIFFLIN HARCOURT

PHOTOGRAPHY CREDITS: 4 (b) ©Radius Images/Corbis; 5 (t) ©Olix Wirtinger/ Fancy/Corbis; 6 (b) ©imagewerks RF/Getty Images; 10 (br) ©Juniors Bildarchiv/ age fotostock; 10 (l) ©Getty Images; 11 (b) ©Litschel/Alamy Images

Printed in Mexico

ISBN: 978-0-544-07229-9

2 3 4 5 6 7 8 9 10 0908 21 20 19 18 17 16 15 14 13

4500456317   A B C D E F G

Contents

Vocabulary	Stretch Vocabulary
engineer	improve
design process	reuse
materials	conserve

Introduction

Sam likes to make things. But he has a problem. His desk is messy!

Sam makes a plan to solve his problem. Next, he makes something to hold his things. He uses an egg carton. He puts things in each space. But they don't fit. Then Sam uses a shoebox. He uses cardboard to divide it into parts. It works!

How would you solve Sam's problem?

An engineer makes a plan, or drawing, of a building.

Engineers Solve Problems

Engineers solve problems. They use math and science. Engineers do many kinds of jobs. Some plan and make buildings and homes. They make sure buildings are safe. Some engineers build safe roads and bridges. They make sure cars, trains, and planes are safe. Some engineers make sure machines work.

It is important to do each step in order. What would happen if an engineer skipped a step?

The Design Process

Engineers follow steps to solve a problem. These steps make up the design process. Here are five steps to follow:

1. Find a Problem
2. Plan and Build
3. Test and Improve
4. Redesign
5. Communicate

Plan and Build a Pet's Home

Mrs. Lee's class is happy. They will be getting a new pet rabbit. Her name is Snowball. But the students have a problem, too. Snowball will need a home. The students want to solve the problem. They will build a home for Snowball.

First, the class begins to make a plan. The children think about what materials they can use to build Snowball's home.

What would you do first to build a home for a rabbit?

Have you ever reused an object to make something new?

The children do not want to buy new materials. They will look for materials that are no longer being used. Then the children will reuse the materials for Snowball's house.

Engineers conserve materials when they build things, too. They try to reuse materials whenever they can.

Make a Plan and Follow It

Ben's dad has some wood that can be reused for Snowball's home.

The children find out how much space a rabbit needs. The children draw a design of the rabbit's new house. The home will fit in the corner of the classroom.

These materials can be used for building a pet's home. What else might you use?

Next, the class builds Snowball's home. The children get help from Ben's dad. They help measure the wood. They measure it two times before it is cut. They do not want to make a mistake. They use an old window screen so that Snowball can see out.

The children look at their plan often. They want to follow it carefully so that Snowball has a wonderful home.

Test, Improve, and Share

The class puts food and water dishes in Snowball's home.

Then, Mrs. Lee puts Snowball into her new home. Snowball hops in the water dish. *Splash!* Then Snowball hops out of her home!

The class improves the home. A top over it keeps Snowball from jumping out. Different containers will conserve food and water.

Which water container will work better for Snowball's home?

It's time to test the home again. Mrs. Lee puts Snowball in her home. Snowball hops around. Snowball can't tip over her food or water. Snowball sniffs her toys. She is happy!

The class is happy, too. They built a nice home for Snowball. Now they will share their plan with other children.

The class made a good plan and followed it.

Draw a Picture

Think of something that needs fixing or improving in your classroom. Discuss with a partner and your teacher. Think of ways to solve the problem. Choose the best solution. Draw a picture of it. Write a caption for your picture. Tell about it.

 ## Write About It

Suppose you had a pet turtle. Think of materials you could reuse to build a home for it. Write a plan for the turtle's new home.